# MR. RIGHT MEETS MISUNDERSTOOD

Michael Banks

and

Shannon Morgan

present...

# Mr. Right MEETS MisUNDERSTOOD

THE KING'S PROJECT

Self Published: Michael Banks and Shannon Morgan

Limits of Liability-Disclaimer

Self-Published

Library of Congress Cataloging-in-Publication Data

Printed in the United States of America.

Cover: Robin L. Miller. Birds Eye View Branding and Design Studio

Editing: Karen A. McCracken and Inspired Editing Services

Interior Layout/Formatting: Joy E. Turner – JetSet Communications & Consulting

ISBN: 978-0-692-57339-6

# Contents

# Part II - Shopping For Love

## Chapter 5

## Chapter 6

## Chapter 7

## Chapter 8

# Dedication

To Maleek. You have proven it is capable to love others
without sacrificing self-love.

# Foreword

**M**r. *Right Meets MisUnderstood* is a book on relationships that presents as a manual to living life. Living life is indeed a relational process. The irony is that we as men and women in relationships find it somewhat difficult to relate to one another. There is a constant struggle of the "individual" versus "we" mentality, which often keeps a couple from dwelling as one.

The authors, Banks and Morgan, have wrestled with different scenarios, and have offered the reader practical knowledge and methods to create a sustainable prescription to lifelong connections while teasing out the interpersonal issues that often erupt along the way. This writing duo is systematic in the way that they untangle the nuisances of male-female encounters. With a sense of purpose, they've created an array of stories that help the reader to actualize and confront the basic pressures in relationships.

These authors have created a brilliant depiction of the mistakes and misconceptions that contaminate our ability to relate authentically in our relationships. What Banks and Morgan discover is surprising in its straightforwardness. Their revelation is good news for those struggling to make sense of their own relationships. This duo, without a doubt, intends to uncover relational skirmishes so that readers can benefit from more harmony and balance in their one-to-one endeavors.

*Mr. Right Meets MisUnderstood* serves as a transformative instrument in reclaiming the beauty and precious nature that relationships were intended to be.

~Bryan Miller, Ph.D.

# Introduction

M ost women would agree with me when I say that we spend way too much time shopping for the "perfect fit." It is our mission to find silky blouses, shape flattering pants, or the quintessential little black dress. But this time ladies, I'm not talking about shopping for that one-of-a-kind body hugging outfit that turns heads. The perfect fit that we spend too much of our time shopping for is that impeccable man who sweeps us off our feet and gives us that textbook romance. Ladies, you know the one! He wows us with his charm and always has us wearing the biggest smile on our faces because we've never been happier.

In our quest for love, we go on relationship shop-ping sprees where we enter in and out of relationships that we had no business entering in the first place. These rela-tionships are toxic. Either they cost us way too much time and energy, or they're cheap and they devalue our worth as women.

This book uses shopping as a witty metaphor for women in search of love. The consequences of shopping in all of the wrong places for all of the wrong reasons will be put on display throughout the next several chapters. My brother and I have created a foolproof master plan that will help transform your methods to find your Mr. Right. So, let's go ladies! We guarantee, your life is about to change!

# Misconceptions Of MisUnderstood

Chapters 1 - 4

Chapter 1

*If* you want different results, you have to work differently.

# 1

## _Shopping In All The Wrong Places_

Relationships that women have no business being in are just like shopping for that perfect gown in a store that can't meet any of their needs or expectations. For example, let's say you are a woman whose goal is to shed some weight; does it really make sense for you to shop in the petite department before achieving your end weight-loss goal? No! That type of thinking is illogical and it's that type of thinking that dooms you from the very beginning in relationships. If you're the woman who has grown tired of the club-hopping knucklehead and have since realized you're more interested in a cultured and professional gentleman, it is unlikely that you will meet him in a dark night club with heavy drinkers and loud music. Location, location, location ladies! Location is key. Shift gears. Find out when the next art exhibit is showcasing, or locate the bar that attracts suit wearing intellects. Learn the names of artists and the difference between red and white wine. Basically, do your homework. Step out of your comfort zone. If you want different results, you have to work differently.

## *Make A List, Check It Twice*

Michael and I want you to understand how important it is to use self-discipline while you are shopping for love. When you are choosing a man to spend your life with, you must be sensible. Finding the right man will be a process that requires self-restraint because it is so easy to give up and settle. In the interim, enjoy the process, love yourself, and believe that you deserve the life you dream of living.

In consideration of the women who are reading this book because they are searching for their perfect fit, we remind you to keep a list of your standards in your Michael Kors Hamilton tote. Michael and I rely on shopping for the perfect look to help you understand your struggle with finding Mr. Right; however, shopping for a cute dress will never measure up to what is required when you are looking for the right man. Do not choose any ole man to spend your time with. Just because you have grown impatient as a result of kissing too many toads, that doesn't mean Prince Charming is an unrealistic option for you.

**You can rush the delivery of your party dress and have it in a day, but you cannot rush the process when looking for the right man.**

## *Don't Worry, Be Happy*

At the end of an arduous journey, everyone's end goal should be happiness. Some women think happiness is meeting a man who is extremely wealthy and other women may say they will be happy for the rest of their lives with someone who is Boris Kodjoe fine. While every woman is entitled to her own ideas of what happiness is, we believe acquiring ultimate happiness in a relationship with your perfect fit is finding that man who complements his woman. This person may be Bill Gates rich, but then again, he may not. The point is this: if he is able to bring out the best in you, then you will remain rich in love and of course, rich in happiness.

Be patient. Work on making smart decisions. If something doesn't make you feel good, then it probably isn't a good idea. Study yourself to learn your needs and wants so that no one can talk you into settling for a man that you know is not able to add to your happiness.

Many women have admitted to entering into relationships with a man who showed who he truly was at the door. Although he wasn't a favorable choice, these women were wishing, hoping, and praying that he might be the perfect example of the the old adage that warns us not to judge a book by its cover. On the day of her official first date with her potential Mr. Right, she is excited and filled with butterflies. She finds it very hard to forget the unpleasant initial encounter with her potential Mr. Right, but since she already agreed to the date, she prays for the best and goes in with her heart and superficial ideals. Before she gives this man a second chance to impress her, she is already hoping he is her dream come true. She has already created a picture perfect romance that includes love, marriage, and a baby carriage. Does that woman sound like you?

Inevitably, this woman has doomed the relationship from the beginning. (1) She ignored her gut reaction to the man when she first met him and (2)she didn't give him an opportunity to prove that he had potential. Shopping in stores that sell items that do not complement you is foolish, just like it's foolish to invest in a man who is not worth your time.

In our book, *Mr. Right Meets MisUnderstood*, we explore three different scenarios with three different women. Each woman's search for a man is presented as if it were a shopping experience. Their world is the mall and the items that they buy represent their potential Mr. Right. Just like women that we already know, these women have very unique sets of circumstances that oftentimes hold them back from experiencing the long-lasting love that they have dreamt of since childhood. We will shed light on the obstacles that inadvertently make up each of these women's personalities with hopes that our readers who have, or are experiencing hardships in finding their perfect fit, will be able to find reliable solutions that correct the recycling of unhealthy dating.

Chapter 2

*I*t is important that you never ever forget that Mr. Right is not responsible for what happened in your relationships before him.

# 2

## A Woman's Heart

How many ways can a woman love a man? There isn't a number; a woman's love is immeasurable. Granted, women do not have agape love, which is the kind of love that never wavers. But women do have the capability to love a man so hard that it makes the ground shake. Yes, it is that deep. A man would have to be transformed into a woman to understand the depth of a woman's affection for him because attempting to explain it would never be enough for a man to comprehend.

You see, in a lot of instances, it only takes one day for a man to make a woman fall deeply in love. If that man says just the right thing, looks at her a certain way, or touches her in the right places, she will end her search in a heartbeat.

On that blissful day, a woman can actually feel her heart drop into her stomach and dance amongst the butterflies. From that point on and moving forward, she is captivated by everything that he does and says even if it's the silliest thing she has ever seen or heard before. He has captured her heart, her mind, and her body; she will pour all of herself into the relationship to ensure his happiness. That is what women live for! They focus on making their man happy; no matter the cost, they are ready to pay it. All they truly hope for is the same in return. To all of the good men, that is the promise of all hopeful women shopping for love. Promises weren't made to be broken, but when a man toys with a woman's heart, that is exactly what happens.

Did this ever happen to you?

# Shannon

## *My Heart Is Closed For Business*

One morning I woke up with big plans to take my acts of love for an ex-boyfriend to a higher level, but wound up going to bed later that night devastated. He broke my heart. Lying against my pillow, I couldn't sleep; but, I was not counting sheep. I was mentally erasing away all of the sweet things that I loved to do for him. He was not going to be the recipient of my love if he couldn't reciprocate my love.

In that moment and for the duration of that relationship, I felt justified in my decision to reduce my demonstration of love. I will admit, the way I felt for my ex-boyfriend did not immediately end when he hurt me, but he was not going to ever find that out. I didn't want him to believe that he could treat me any kind of way and still receive my heart. Choosing to continue in that relationship with that type of attitude was isolating. He no longer felt like my best friend. Being his girlfriend went from being on cloud nine to being placed in solitary confinement. He and I continued to act like a normal couple. We went on dates, shared events from our day, and were still intimate (minus the passion); that gradually lessened until our relationship was over.

The decision to limit my love for him was unwork -able in that relationship. I'm not saying that I should have given him a second chance to break my heart; however, what I understand now is that limiting my acts of love to almost zilch for my ex did me more of a disservice. I sincer- ely wanted to give my Mr. Right all of my love over teaching him a hard lesson.

For a woman, it is just as easy to feel heartbreak as it is to feel herself falling in love. Ask any woman who had her heart broken before and she will be sure to tell you that it feels like someone stole her spirit. A woman is left empty on the inside. She feels like she's been run over by Cupid himself, and left on the side of the road as if she was love's roadkill. She wants nothing more than her old self back, but she has been robbed of her joy and no longer knows what her old self feels like.

My experience temporarily changed who I was intended to be: loving, loyal, forgiving, and understanding - no matter what! The pain was too much for me to bear. I knew immediately after his indiscretion that he was not my Mr. Right. I should have moved on.

I didn't though.

I became MisUnderstood. The ruins of a heartbreak tragedy. I built skyscraping walls. I needed to be certain no man could reach my heart because in my mind, love was now an obligation, not a gift. I fought the natural urge to be vulnerable in my relationships that would follow until I was bulletproof. For years to come, I would find it difficult to be what a man wanted and needed. Even though I fantasized about being everything a man could dream of (loving, giving, compromising, and considerate), my abilities were weighed down by baggage that I picked up in my previous relationship, hence the title, *Mr. Right Meets MisUnderstood*.

## *How MisUnderstood Shops*

Imagine this: After you leave the grocery store, you decide to stop at the mall to buy yourself something new. Once you arrive at the mall, you take the grocery bags with you. You are now in the mall shopping with grocery bags in your hand.

Who does that!?

In the mall, you are looking for a new dress, a pair of boots, and some new slacks for work. Carrying around all of those extra bags from the supermarket will do nothing but weigh you down, make your shopping experience less enjoyable, and overall ruin what was supposed to be an opportunity to treat yourself to something new.

Now, imagine leaving a relationship and looking to enter into a new one. You were exclusively dating a man we will call Tony. During the relationship, Tony cheated on you, mentally abused you, and no matter how hard he claimed he tried, he always failed at showing you the kind of love that you truly deserved. It took some courage, but finally, you left Tony alone. Still wanting to find companionship, you go on a shopping spree for love. On this shopping spree, you hope to find someone who is loyal, honest, and fun to be around; but with every guy you meet, you notice that the baggage you acquired from your relationship with Tony keeps getting in the way.

One of your bags holds your inability to be loved by someone. David, a new potential Mr. Right, says he really likes you but you find it very hard to trust him because you won't forget how Tony was unable to show you love. Another bag holds your idea that all men are cheaters. Well, David also says he is looking to settle down with you; yet, you can't be so sure because Tony cheated on you with almost every woman in town.

Just like you unnecessarily carried those grocery bags into the supermarket, you unnecessarily carried the baggage from your old relationship with Tony into your new relationship with David. David has what you are looking for in a man, but you can't focus on his strengths because you're unable to let go of Tony's faults.

Now, who does that?

It is important that you never ever forget that Mr. Right is not responsible for what happened in your relationships before him. With all that being said, if you see yourself in our example, do you think you are mentally and emotionally ready for love?

Before you start chapter three of our book, commit yourself to showing love to a person that is normally difficult for you to deal with. This person could be your spouse who never helps around the house. This person could be your neighbor who never greets you. This person could be a relative that you never got along with, or even an old friend that you grew apart from. This person could be you.

If you identify with MisUnderstood's behavior, acknowledge it today. MisUnderstood is not who you were intended to become; therefore, underneath that pain is a loving spirit lying dormant. Get ready to fearlessly release all the love that lives deep inside of you. You deserve to be freed from your hurt. Let go and let love lift you higher.

Chapter 3

*B*aggage: Any character trait or flaw that was developed in a previous relationship and has the potential to negatively impact a current or future relationship.

# 3

## Bag Lady

In the next few chapters, you will read about three different women who are looking for love in spite of their baggage. Inside of those bags, each woman holds her individual insecurities. Whatever those insecurities are and from whatever time they were developed, these inhibitions were given permission to exist, and now these women are scarred by the pain that their past relationships have caused.

Unknowingly, some women hold tightly to their baggage and they are the women they have become because of what they have been carrying around. In some cases this can be a victory as pain sometimes paves the way for purpose. But what about those women who did not gain from their pain? Instead of finding strength, they have become weaker.

And now the pain speaks for those women instead of those women speaking against their pain.

We have met many women and embraced them because of their keen differences. We have also observed the common theme that connects them: they all want to find love. But what we've learned during our research that many women have not, is that women oftentimes allow preexisting baggage to block the opportunity for real love to enter. Thorough scrutiny on this subject has revealed that before finding love in a man, a woman must start with finding love for herself.

The phrase 'love yourself' is widely used, but what is the specific meaning? After finding an understanding of what love truly is, we've found to love yourself simply means to invest in yourself. Women are famously known for going out of their way to show someone love. They invest in their children, boyfriends or spouses, friends, family members, co-workers, and even strangers. A woman's ability to love so many unconditionally, is marvelous. Unfortunately, women are not always rewarded because of this amazing attribute, but they still find it hard to fight wanting to make people happy.

To those women who show love endlessly and never get a return on their investment, it is time to sit those people in the backseat for a minute. You have spread so much love for everyone around you and forgot to keep a little love at home. You may feel guilty about this at first, but we guarantee you won't regret showing yourself more love than you could ever ask for.

## Acts Of Self-Love

Forgiveness: Let go of the pain from mistakes that were either self-inflicted or caused by others. Those indescretions may have left a bad impression on your heart, but letting go will enable you to make peace with yourself as well as others.

Look Good: Put an obvious effort into your looks. This does not mean you have to wear designer clothes and shoes or be draped in diamonds and fur; this simply means you should be well-groomed at all times. If you cannot afford to have a hair stylist – no problem! There are enough YouTube videos on the internet to have you styling like a pro.

Positive Attitude: Smile more! Avoid gossip. Stay away from people who are negative; their bad attitudes are like colds. Negativity is a sickness that's contagious and if you sit around it too long, you will catch it.

Set Boundaries: Stop allowing people to intrude with their questions and opinions. Do you have the friend who's always inquiring about your relationship with questions or unwanted suggestions that sound like, "When are you getting married," or "If I were you, I wouldn't..." It's okay to tell people to mind their business, in a nice way of course. Here's how: "I like the way everything is going for me as it is," or you could say, "Your concern is appreciated but your suggestions aren't needed."

Health and Wellness: Maintaining your physical and mental health is a struggle; nonetheless, they are important hurdles to overcome. People who have a clean bill of health and a clear mind function more effectively.

Enjoy Yourself: Do the things you like to do and feel good about it.

## *Take Control*

After speaking with a variety of women, they have admitted to being in countless relationships that showed no promise, and although it hurt, they stayed. Why? Well, they stayed because those women relied on men to keep them happy; therefore, it didn't make any sense to leave only to be lonely and in pain. Their rationalization for not leaving those unfulfilled relationships was (1) they were chosen (they felt pretty and special) and (2) they knew him (but even with the one you "know," you will never really know what to expect from that person day after day). Those women were comfortable and familiar with the way those men made them feel even though the feeling hurt so badly. And because they strongly believed that all men were the same, those women felt no need to search for what they thought would be some new kind of disappointment.

Does this woman sound like you?

It didn't take those women long to realize that those men would never make them happy. For the ones who wanted a change in their relationship and most importantly, believed there could be a positive change, they told us they asked for help. Seeking help saved some of their relationships and it saved most of their lives. They gained wisdom, and eventually they began to understand that it was solely their responsibility to find security in one thing — self-awareness. They realized that if they never took the time to appreciate themselves and love who they are as an individual, they would never lead a happy life, even if God dropped the perfect man into their laps. You must pursue self discovery passionately to have resolve and peace. It may be challenging to accept your imperfections and take responsibility for the role you played in the downfall of your past relationships; nevertheless, stay committed to the assignment.

There were times that Shannon and I became frustrated after talking to countless women about how they cannot find their Mr. Right. There are so many Mr. Wrong stories out here, we have lost track of the number. The same chorus line in the Mr. Wrong song is, "Will men ever change?" But like the Michael Jackson song, *Man In the Mirror* suggests, if you want a change, you must start with yourself. We have witnessed the misunderstood woman enter into a courtship with a man while she is unsure of her own identity. All the while, she expects this man to fully understand her and love her. Ladies, that is a difficult feat for a man dating a woman who is carrying around a bag of secrets. MisUnderstood is either afraid to deal with her issues or is not aware she is hampered by them. Oblivious to how affected she is by her shortcomings, MisUnderstood goes shopping for Mr. Right.

1.  What issues from your past do you believe are holding you back from true happiness?

_____

_____

_____

_____

_____

_____

_____

2.  What insecurities negatively influence your relationship?

_____

_____

_____

_____

_____

_____

_____

_____

3.  How were these insecurities created?

_____

_____

_____

_____

_____

_____

_____

# Chapter 4

Don't be a knock-off version
of your authentic self.

# 4

## Baggage Claim

As explained in chapter three, it is extremely important to discover who you are so that you can authentically present and showcase yourself to your Mr. Right. What sense does it make to lose out on what you always dreamt of just because bags keep getting in the way?

I do realize that it can be challenging to just be yourself if you don't actually understand who you are as a woman. The key to understanding is acknowledging. You mustn't be afraid of acknowledging your strengths and your weaknesses - we all have them. We carry these traits around with us almost daily. Some of these traits are like your life-line, some of them are reserved for special occasions like an interview and some of these traits just magically appear-those can be lifesavers or deal breakers. But again, no one is perfect. Issues - we all have them. Even the "total package" has something that is flawed in the eyes of another human being. That's just life. There are too many people living to seem altogether when there is no such thing. Under our arms there are bags, some are heavy and some are light. The heavier bags are usually our deepest and darkest secrets or our biggest issues to face. The lighter bags are more like the events or issues in our life that had an impact, but the impact wasn't destructible. Nevertheless, the bags are there and it's about time that we claim them.

From experience, I didn't want to claim my baggage because I thought I would appear less desirable to the guy I was dating. I really liked him and I didn't want to mess that up with revealing that I was not the quality lady he thought I was. Instead, deep down I felt like I was just a Bargain Basic and he did not catch himself "the item of the day." Later on, I realized that I was happy with not being the trend of the season. Trends come and go, they may revisit, but they are not a staple item. Staples last forever. They have a quality and charm about them that will never die. In the world of love to be considered a staple piece, you must be an honest woman.

Start releasing your baggage by uncovering where the bags came from. The first step in the process of uncovering is acknowledging your baggage. Up until now, these bags have been strongholds and hindrances because you unknowingly carried them with you daily. Once you acknowledge your baggage, it will become easy to move to the next step which is identifying what provokes the feeling(s) attached to them.

Think about an unpleasant experience. Try to remember the feelings that experience left you with. In the space provided below, take note of those feelings and how they have affected you, especially in your relationships and your self esteem.

_____

_____

_____

_____

_____

_____

_____

_____

_____

_____

_____

_____

## Reveal Your Baggage

Unfortunately, we live in a world where people live their lives in a way that appears they've got it altogether, but there is no such thing as being altogether. Perpetrating the perfect woman because you have yet to claim your baggage will not get you what you deserve in a relationship with your perfect fit. Being a knock-off version of your authentic self is selling your potential Mr. Right a dream that will be crushed once you step out of character.

Revealing your baggage is done through having a conversation about all of your insecurities. It is also exposed through your actions. A bag lady is spotted from miles away. It's the slouch in her shoulders that says, "I'm not important," or it's the attitude in her voice that screams, "I don't know how to be loved."

A bag lady doesn't have to tell a man that she is scarred from her previous relationships. Her body language roars like a lion and she will be heard. Ironically, most men don't mind the bag lady because men are designed to fix problems. Having any opportunity to make their woman feel better is a plus in most men's book of accomplishments; but in order for men to help their woman feel better, they need to know what the problem is. Most women that we've spoken to realized this fact about men; nevertheless, they still keep their baggage a secret. This is because women are afraid of being judged by their male counterparts. We know telling you to get over it is easier for us to say than for you to do, but eventually, you will need to get over the fear of being judged. Start by loving yourself. No matter how cliché that may sound, loving yourself is more than half of the battle. If you truly love yourself, you should understand that what you have gone through are just experiences, not a depiction of your character. So, when a man asks a question, answer it honestly or you'll never know what will come from being a sincere woman.

## *The Shopping Experience*

It has been known that women love to shop. What's most important about shopping is the shopping experience.

**The Shopping Experience — a process that you go through when looking for Mr. Right.**

For example, some things you may encounter are:

- Dating
  - o Speed Dating
  - o Serial Dating
  - o Blind Dating
  - o Online Dating

- Flirting - casually entertaining a person that you find attractive or is attracted to you
- Sex

- o     Casual Sex
- o     One Night Stand
- o     Friends with Benefits
- Previous Relationships
  - o     Ex-boyfriend
  - o     Ex-husband
  - o     The one that got away
  - o     An old fling

**BEWARE: Some of these experiences can interfere with finding your Mr. Right.**

The thrill and excitement of having something new is always a great feeling; still, it is possible for this experience to be hindered by collecting too many bags along the way. Picture yourself in the mall making several different purchases from several different stores and now you have multiple bags in your hand. The room for more is getting smaller and smaller. Some stores have acknowledged the joy of shopping, so they've created a generous policy, which is check your bags at the door. What does that mean? Some of you may be thinking the salesperson wants to be sure you won't steal. While that may be true, that theory is not always the case. The store manager may presume that shoppers have acquired some baggage as a result of shopping from store to store; therefore, they anticipate the potential hindrance that may come along with carrying around too many bags at one time, ergo their check your bags policy.

Entering a new relationship is just the same as entering a new store. Meeting different men and getting the chance to know them through exciting dates is a thrill. Still, you will carry baggage from past relationships into your new ones, which in most cases gets in the way of fully enjoying the company of your potential Mr. Right. Because some women have carried their baggage around for so long it is likely they will not realize that those bags are causing a problem. Just like the sales clerk who only intended to make your shopping experience pleasurable, meeting a new man is the same. Men call women out to bring attention to an insecurity that is getting in the way of the relationship experience. Instead of becoming offended by a mans honesty, take responsibility, and check your bags.

**Check Your Bags:  Acknowledging and addressing any issues that you have before entering into a relationship. Any unresolved issues that you have before the relationship will inevitably become a problem during the relationship.**

Ladies, never forget that men are well aware that you are carrying baggage. In most cases, you will not be the first "bag lady" your potential Mr. Right has dated. He already knows what you have in store for him and he understands it is not always going to be a picnic in the park. Nonetheless, men still seek love hoping to find that one special woman. There is no amount of baggage in the world that would make a man stay away from the girl of his dreams. So when you find your Mr. Right, check your bags at the door. Don't let the fear of being vulnerable interfere with your relationship. You must possess some level of trust. Let Mr. Right handle you with care.

*#CheckWhatsWrongWithYouBeforeYouWreckWhosRightForYou*

1. Can you acknowledge at least two instances where you allowed your baggage to negatively affect a promising relationship?

_____

_____

_____

_____

_____

_____

_____

2. Are you afraid to reveal your baggage? If so, why?

_____

_____

_____

_____

_____

_____

_____

3. What are some methods that you use to reveal your baggage in a relationship?

_____

_____

_____

_____

_____

_____

_____

4. It is important that you know your strengths. List at least three strengths that can positively affect an intimate relationship.

_____

_____

_____

_____

_____

_____

_____

# Shopping For Love

## Chapters 5 - 8

Chapter 5

*D*on't allow the attraction to
be the distraction.

# 5

## Trials Of Tracey

Tracey thought that shopping was her sport. She knew what she was looking for and she knew the mall would have just what she wanted.

Picture this: Tracey and her friends are at the mall perusing the many options. After her friends find exactly what they are looking for, they begin to pressure Tracey to make a decision. Tracey decides to settle on one item. The color is right, but the fit is a little off. Tracey's friends had already found dresses that fit them just right and though Tracey was unsure about making the purchase, her friends insisted that it was a great bargain because it was on sale. Deep down Tracey knew that purchasing the dress was a bad idea, but with her friends in her ear, she decides to make it work. Although the dress didn't make Tracey jump for joy, she wondered if she had anything to lose? It was really pretty and it was on sale, so she could afford to get it tailored to fit her just right. Tracey bought the dress.

## Settling For Less

Ladies, how many times have you been in Tracey's situation and settled for less than what you really deserve? In your heart, you desire glitter and gold, but somehow you always end up with rusty copper. Why is that?

There are several reasons why women settle, but we want to focus on just two of those reasons. Women settle because they believe they are not good enough and for the sake of contentment. These are the top two reasons why the women who want to find their Mr. Right always end up with Mr. Wrong. If you believe you are not good enough, then you will never achieve the best that life has to offer. Destroy the idea that you are inadequate by choosing to pursue the best of the best.

**Challenge Yourself - Commit to doing something bold everyday and be sure to track your moves.**

## Take The Wheel

When you are searching for love and companionship, you should be the only person in control of the outcome. The road becomes longer and detours start to arise when you become a passenger and put others in the driver seat. We believe the popular catch phrase is, "Jesus take the wheel," not, "Mama take the wheel," or "BFF take the wheel."

You don't ever reach your desired destination because you're too busy letting others give you direction. Every woman has her own process and preference when she is searching for love; be careful not to adopt another woman's method as your own. Instead, you should adhere to your own ideals because what worked for your mama may not necessarily work for you. This is a problem that some of you make in your everyday life. You seek counsel, wisdom, or advice from people who you know can't help you on your journey. This is not to discredit these relationships, but you have to learn how to love people at the level they're on. It's okay to be friends, but don't ask this friend to set you up on a blind date with a guy who's heavily involved in church when all she usually dates are thugs.

## *Pay Attention To Your Intentions*

**Everything that looks good to you isn't always good for you.**

We've realized that most of the time we question a person's intention, but the intention in question should be our own. What are your intentions for yourself? Do you feel you are missing something and that is why you mistakenly invest in men who don't complement you?

Before embarking on the shopping spree for love, you must acknowledge and respect your intentions. Never lose focus! Your intent is to find your Mr. Right and you are the only one who can control the outcome of your goal. Searching for love is not an easy task, but the only way to be successful is to be patient and intuitive.

## *Patience*

If you currently struggle with patience, it is time to finally work out those kinks. Patience is a tool that is used to build your dreams. Without patience, what do you expect to create? Lack of patience only produces undesired results, yet so many of us can't fight the need for immediate gratification. Ask yourself, "How badly do you want to find your Mr. Right?" Then ask yourself, "What am I willing to do to get him?"

You should never force a relationship with a man. A move like that is a set-up for failure. If he doesn't seem like a potential perfect fit, then he is not your Mr. Right. There are three stages in all relationships: the honeymoon stage (the beginning), the comfortable stage (the middle), and the love-hate stage (the rest of your life). If you are working hard at making it work from the start you will never get a chance to experience the most enchanting stage in the whole relationship - the beginning.

Letting go of patience seats you in relationships that aren't in your favor. There are many reasons why people grow impatient with being alone, and of all the many justifi-cations, none of them are good reasons for abandoning your patience. Hastily entering into a relationship with a man that obviously does not fit you will never work.

Making impulsive dating commitments have the same effect as buyer's remorse. You'll be the first person in line trying to get a refund because you took the dress home and realized it was never the right choice in the first place. Aside from the time you'll waste returning the ill-fitting dress, impulsive purchases aren't as life altering as picking the wrong man. Just remember, it's not so easy exchanging one man for a better one.

## Intuitiveness

**If you know upfront that a man doesn't measure up to your standards, do not let him enter your life.**

Many women are just like Tracey. They are initially drawn to someone based on how they look. Interestingly enough, you do know when you shouldn't let certain peo-ple into your life, yet you neglect your own intelligence and welcome trouble. You put your hopes in the intentions that someone else has for you. Let's swap Tracey's shopping ex-perience for a second. Instead of Tracey shopping for a dress, she was shopping for love. In Tracey's case, she was able to immediately determine that the guy wasn't her perfect fit. Despite that fact, Tracey moved forward and exchanged numbers with him, allowing her attraction to him to distract her from her better judgement. The pressure from her friends didn't make the decision any easier.

**Never be impressed by a man who is only able to get your attention;** *keeping* **your attention is more important.**

Tracey thought that she would be able to get the uncomfortable, ill-fitting dress tailored to fit her just right. That is a major mistake made in shopping and just like in relationships, dating a man that is not your perfect fit is an unpleasant circumstance for any woman. That type of decision is highly discouraged.

If you haven't learned by now, we are here to tell you that you cannot change a man. There is no amount of money, cooking, sex, or lies a woman can tell a man to make him act right. It is his responsibility as a man to treat his woman with respect. If he fails, send him back where he came from. Your intuition will always remind you of your original intentions. Listening is the key.

**Don't allow the attraction to be the distraction.**

1. What is your shopping style when you're looking for love?

> A. Snatch up the first thing that looks good.
>
> B. Snatch up the first thing that shows interest in you.
>
> C. Take your time to make sure there is a connection.

2. Have you ever dated or entertained a man that you knew wasn't a good fit for you in the very beginning? If so, why?

_____

_____

_____

_____

_____

3. What type of men are you attracted to?

_____

_____

_____

_____

4. What kind of men do you attract?

_____

_____

_____

_____

_____

_____

_____

_____

5. If the answer to number 4 is inconsistent with the answer to number 3, what are the reasons why?

_____

_____

_____

_____

_____

_____

_____

## *Company Versus Companion*

As we search for our perfect fit we hope to find companionship, so it's extremely important that you recognize when you are being used for company. This subject may be a delicate topic to address, but the truth heals.

Shannon and I understand there may be a need for company when you are going through the process of finding your companion. We are human; therefore, it's natural to yearn for healthy interactions with whom you are instinctively attracted to, but what are your intentions with this person? And what are their intentions for you? Are your intentions to be platonic and just do lunch every now and then? Or are you most interested in building a long-term commitment?

We've noticed that women don't realize the power they have in relationships with men. Ladies, once you realize what a man's intentions are, make your move. Whether his heart is in the right place and he wants to seriously get to know you or he is just looking for a booty call, you are the determining factor of where that relationship will go - not him. Be careful not to treat your company like your companion.

Don't give temporary people a permanent position in your life. Let them serve their purpose and leave. When you allow people who were only meant to fulfill a temporary assignment stick around longer than what was intended, you will consequently become a victim of their ways. This is why distinguishing *company* versus *companion* is very important.

My very first girlfriend should have been the one that got away - and quickly! I was a natural disaster bound to destroy any woman in my path. I was so intoxicated the night that we met that it should have been a crime for me to be walking. But the only crime that I committed was a crime of the heart.

The night of our meet and greet, we were amongst a group of mutual friends, but we were the only single souls there. For me, my ex was merely entertainment that night. She attempted to converse with me, but my lines were slurred and very hard to understand. I asked for her number because it was the guy thing to do, not because I was really interested in her.

Two days later my phone rang. It was her. What a surprise! Actually, I wasn't surprised. And let me remind you, I did nothing at all except for act like a complete fool. I was less than a gentleman and I gained her interest. That wasn't hard for me and because I was so screwed up back then, it was easy to execute the mistreatment throughout our entire relationship. If she would've paid attention to her intentions (pg 49), she probably wouldn't have ended up with the loser I once was. Her decision to kick it with me was made because of self-imposed peer pressure. Nevertheless, she was impatient and couldn't wait to find a companion.

Ladies, you must know your strengths and weaknesses. For example, if you know that you have a severe shopping problem, it may not be the wisest decision to hang out with the girlfriend who likes to shop just as much as you do. Likewise, if you're waiting on Mr. Right, don't place yourself in a predicament that causes you to compromise your end goal.

For my ex, I was company (bad company at that) and that was it. After the weekend had passed and after careful consideration, she actually thought that I had potential to offer her companionship. I treated her badly and I am not proud of that by any means, which is why I encourage you to be patient and intuitive. Finding your Mr. Right is not a quest that you should rush through or take jokingly. Dating is fun and getting to be around someone new can be even more fun, but those sparks do eventually fizzle. It's important to be almost certain that this man is tolerable when things are going good and when they are bad.

Overall, Tracey's issue was that she was too quick to settle. Tracey was open for business to anyone who wanted to enter into her life. She made herself available even when she knew that the something or someone was not good for her at all. Tracey simply needed to recognize that she was worthy of being treated like a queen.

**Shopping for a spouse is equivalent to shopping for a new outfit. You shouldn't spend money on something you can't afford, so don't spend time with a man who can't afford you.**

If you see yourself in Tracey, remedy the problem by treating yourself like the royalty that you are. Stop waiting for a man to do for you what you already have the power to do for yourself. In what ways do you treat yourself like royalty? If you cannot identify any areas in your life where you treat yourself special, then jot down things that you would like to do for yourself.

_____

_____

_____

_____

_____

_____

_____

_____

_____

_____

_____

_____

_____

_____

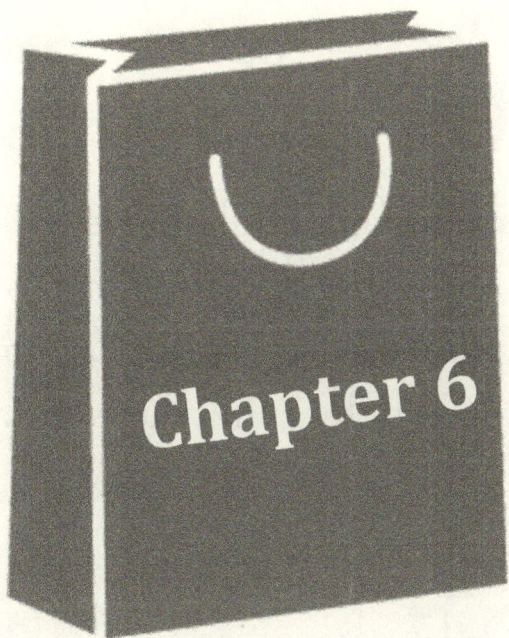

Chapter 6

Using manipulation is a one-sided approach in a two-sided partnership that will undoubtedly ruin your bond.

# 6

## *Erica's Errors*

In chapter six, we would like you to meet Erica. Erica spends a lot of her time shopping, so she is bound to find the perfect pair of shoes. In the past, Erica experienced many nice shoes, but one particular pair purchased was a hot commodity.

The Christian Louboutins.

All ladies dream of the chance to wear Christian Louboutins, but shoes like these are exclusive, and not easy to get your hands on. Eventually, Erica's prayers were answered as she finally found the shoes of her dreams. Erica was finally satisfied because her wardrobe was now complete.

For a little while, Erica treasured her new Christian Louboutins because she knew they would never fail her. She made sure to walk lightly so that they wouldn't crease and to hop over cracks in the sidewalk to avoid scuffing the backs of the heels. She got them shined once the leather started to look weathered and placed them carefully in the box after every wear. Erica was the proud owner of her first pair of designer heels and nothing could ever take their place. They were perfect in every way.

A few months passed and the novelty began to wear off. Erica's love for her shoes started to wane. Erica would race up several flights of stairs when she was running late for a meeting and she would kick the shoes off of her feet as soon as she stepped into her home. The care that she once had for her shoes dwindled and everyone around her could see it. Erica's friends reminded her that those shoes are every woman's dream. "If you're not going to take good care of them, give them to me. I know how to love a good pair of shoes," one friend warned.

"Why are you treating them like that," her mom would ask.

So back to the mall Erica went. Erica purchased new blouses, skirts, dresses, and pants in efforts to prove that she could love the Christian Louboutins the same way she did when she was only admiring them on display. When that plan didn't work, she started shopping for lace, fishnet, and sheer stockings hoping to remedy the problem in that way. Unfortunately, Erica's manipulative attempts to reignite her interest failed. Erica's insatiable appetite to discover something better overpowered her. And despite what her mother and friends all said, Erica wanted to move on. She had her eyes on another pair of shoes that she thought were even more exclusive than her Christian Louboutins. These shoes were very extravagant. They were embellished with precious stones and had a shiny finish. They were beautiful indeed, but they could not be worn season to season and they did not complement every outfit like the Christian Louboutins could. Blinded by the season's newest trend, Erica bought the shoes.

After the summer months ended, Erica had no choice but to retire her new, beautiful shoes; they were not built to weather the rain, sleet, hail, or snow. Those beautiful shoes were only good for showing off on sunny days. Erica secretly felt ashamed of her thoughtless decision to waste her hard-earned money on those expensive shoes since she only got to wear them for three months. In desperate need of a shoe durable to withstand every climate, beautiful enough to wear for any occasion, and that would complete her wardrobe, Erica remembers her Christian Louboutins. She reaches in the back of her closet for the Christian Louboutins to discover they were ruined due to her lack of care for them. It was in that moment that Erica wished she would have appreciated them more.

Erica wants to fall in love with the man of her dreams, get married, and create a family. But she doesn't see how her lack of appreciation interferes with a relationship that's already great. Erica's belief is, there is always more that her man can do to make her feel special. So even after he whisked Erica away on an all expense paid vacation, Erica was dissatisfied because she wasn't able to buy souvenirs for her family and friends. Erica always devalued her man's efforts to make her happy. So what ultimately ends up happening is Erica's Mr. Right began to do less for her. Erica's lack of appreciation has made him feel that he is damned if he do and damned if he don't. So why bother?

Although Erica finally found a guy that would be classified by most women as the perfect fit, he was not the right fit for her. Some women are lucky to find their knight in shining armor - a gentleman who is willing and ready to take care of his woman and treat her like a queen. But because Erica was hard to please, she could not see the beauty in the man that would give her the world.

*Shannon*

## The Honeymoon Stage

In the beginning, we are always excited about the honeymoon stage. This is the period in your relationship when everything is perfect. There are no fights, only cute disagreements, we enjoy all of our companions interests (even activities that we hate), we always want to be around him, we'll call in sick just to be with him, he is the smartest and funniest man in the world, we reference him in all of our conversations with our girlfriends, and we only have eyes for him. He is the epitome of the idiom, "God's gift." But before you know it, a significant amount of time has passed and the love doesn't feel like it did in the beginning. Our cute disagreements turn into huge arguments. We start to notice those physical imperfections that magically hid themselves for months. We turn down all invitations to partake in his favorite hobbies. And we hardly bring his name up in conversations with our girlfriends. He has officially plucked our last nerve and we begin to anticipate the lifespan of the relationship. We start to lose appreciation for our man because our expectations conflict with our reality. And the reality is all relationships are going to experience highs and lows. The highs are undoubtedly exciting, but going through the lows and enduring them just make our next round of highs even more exciting than the time before.

The change in Erica's disposition is so common in many women who are exiting the honeymoon phase of their relationship. To gain control over their new and seemingly unfortunate state, women will resort to using manipulation in their relationship to either have their Mr. Right feel guilty or to get their way. Using manipulation is a one-sided approach in a two-sided partnership that will undoubtedly ruin your bond.

## Manipulation Versus Appreciation

**Manipulation - when you intentionally attempt to control a person or a situation by using underhanded tactics so that it will benefit you in the end**

I don't know about you ladies, but I was not shy about using what I got to get what I wanted in my relationship. When I was super insecure, all I could think about was the possibility of my man cheating on me with other women. I didn't like for my man to hang out with his brothers or any of his friends. He had never been unfaithful to me, but because men in the past were, I believed that he couldn't be any different. The only way to protect my heart and the windows of his car, was to make him stay home.

In the very beginning, we would argue, which didn't resolve anything. Either he would stay in the house (with an attitude) or he would leave and I would worry, cry, and send hateful texts until he came home. I realized that was a lose-lose for me, so I went another route.

Sexy lingerie, home-cooked meals, and new video games were all apart of my arsenal to manipulate him into staying home. For a long while my collection of weaponry was effective. But when I was doing everything in my power to stop him from celebrating his brother's birthday, the you-know-what hit the fan. My tactic was revealed and he was disgusted. We didn't break-up, but for a long time, he was not very happy in our relationship. He paid me little to no attention most of the time. Whenever I would try to converse with him, his responses were short. In case you haven't guessed, his new behavior made me even more insecure. I was living my worst nightmare and it was no one's fault but my own.

I wanted to have a strong relationship, but I knew that without trust, our union would be miserable or short-lived. I didn't want that to be my outcome. I knew in my heart that I had found a good man and it was my own insecurities that were jeopardizing our future together. So I let my guards down and revealed all of my baggage to him. He was surprised that I compared him to other men from my past who had no good intentions for me from the start. His only intention for me was to make me happy and he proved that to be true from the first day we met.

Having that honest conversation with my man made a world of difference in our relationship. I didn't resolve my trust issues overnight, but because I made a choice to believe in him, my trust grew until I had no more worries.

## Appreciation - when your love is based around who they are to you and not what they do for you

In many ways Erica is no different from you and me. We give social standards the power to manipulate our own standards. How many times have you found the one and then made him feel guilty because he wasn't performing like another woman's man? I won't lie. I have.

My experience went like this: My man made me smile every single day up until I realized that he wasn't doing for me what my friend's man was doing for her. In my opinion, my friend's relationship was so much better than mine. She and her man vacationed out of the country, had date night oftentimes in a week, and he bought her nice gifts. I felt like I deserved to be treated the same. The spark that me and my man had was extinguished because of my envy.

After some time, I learned that my friend's relationship wasn't just what I saw. There was behind the scenes drama that I wasn't privy of until that one day she needed to vent. On that day I learned that my friend's "perfect fit" cheated on her religiously, lied habitually, and to her dismay, fathered another woman's child. She was at her wits end.

I was in shock. I couldn't believe that the smiling couple posted all over social media was concealing so much hurt. I felt so bad for my friend, but I felt even worse for my man. I made my man feel terrible about not living up to what another man could do as if that other man was perfect. The reality is that my man was and still is perfect for me. In addition to all that he did for me back then, he was always loyal and still is. I wouldn't replace his faithfulness for any trip or pair of shoes in the world.

Before I learned that the grass was not greener in my friend's backyard, I tried to manipulate my man into being a better man. And because he truly loved me, he did his best to up the ante. But it really didn't matter what he did to be better, I still didn't appreciate his efforts. I always demanded more, so I kept raising the bar.

I was such a fool and so ungrateful. Our love was just as it was supposed to be - unique. Thank God, I was enlightened before it was too late.

## *How To Appreciate Your Mr. Right*

At one time I was only interested in what my man could do for me. It was so bad that I didn't even know how to pick out a birthday gift for him. I took no interest in learning about his favorite things or wildest dreams. When his birthday came around and he opened up a gift wrapped box of socks, his sad 'thank you' crushed me. I failed him. It was the disappointment across his face that showed me how selfish I was. This man did anything I asked of him without hesitation; the least I could do for him was show my appreciation.

Most men are easy to please. Sometimes you just need to simply:

- Say the words "I appreciate you."

- Say 'thank you.' This is important for your man to hear because it reassures him that you're appreciative for him being in your life.

- Give a compliment. Men need to feel wanted just as much as women. Let your Mr. Right know that you're attracted to him.

- Do something nice just because; this will let your Mr. Right know that you're not just on the receiving end of the relationship. Don't just celebrate him on holidays, birthdays, Christmas, and Valentine's Day. Celebrate him just because it's Monday. This will show your Mr. Right that you think of him just as much as he thinks of you.

1.  When is the last time you did something nice for your Mr. Right?

_____

_____

_____

2.  List some instances where you went out of your way to show your appreciation for your Mr. Right.

_____

_____

_____

3.  When are you most prone to show your love and affection for Mr. Right?

     A.      Birthdays

     B.      Holidays (Christmas and Valentine's Day)

     C.      Random occasions just because he's special

     D.      Only A and B

     E.      After he does something nice for you

     F.      In the bedroom (you may get a pass for this one)

     G.      All of the above

## *The Power Couple*

Even though the highs are action packed twenty-four seven, the lows are what transforms the cute couple into the power couple.

Immediately, you probably thought of Beyonce and Jay Z. They are quite the team. But you don't have to be mega rich or a superstar to attain power couple status with your Mr. Right, all you have to do is:

- Be Ready: Enjoy all of the great moments that are going to occur in your relationship because there will be some trying moments peppered in there.

- Be a Fighter: Refuse to allow outside influences interfere with your relationship.

- Treat your relationship like it's VIP: Keep your relationship just between the two of you; your bond is sacred and you should treat it as such.

- Be of Love: Practice being loving towards your Mr. Right; love conquers all.

- Be Supportive: Your Mr. Right is going to be strong, but when he is feeling weak, you must be there to build him up with love, patience, and kindness.

- Be Open: Your Mr. Right may be from a different world than what you are accustomed to; trust that what he has to offer will be a learning experience your relationship will benefit from.

- Listen More Than You Talk: Listening is the only way you will master the art of loving your Mr. Right.

- Make Loving Your Mr. Right A Priority: Life happens, but don't let that stop the way you deliver your love to your man.

Chapter 7

Discover your man's strengths and learn to appreciate him for his qualities rather than forcing him to wear shoes that don't fit.

# 7

## Farrah's Flaws

**M**eet Farrah. She is desperate to find a head-to-toe look that is to die for, but always ends at square one because of her constant nitpicking. Farrah has an eye for high fashion, so picking the perfect look is an effortless task. Farrah is very sensible; therefore, even though she knows that her outfit is a head turner she still heads to the fitting room to confirm her impression with a once-over in the mirror. Even after she has confirmed that the whole outfit looks great to wear, Farrah needs a second, third, and fourth opinion. She steps out of the fitting room and asks the sales associates for their thoughts on her look. After she is given the thumbs up from them all, Farrah heads to the cashier and hesitantly purchases the outfit and the shoes.

Once Farrah gets home from the mall, she tries on the whole look again. She walks around in the shoes and twirls around in the clothes because she needs to be sure that they feel just right. Once her friends come over to pick her up, Farrah asks for their opinion about her outfit. They all tell her how much they love the way she looks, but for some reason Farrah is still hesitant about wearing her new look out with her friends. The blouse fits perfectly. It is a beautiful color that makes her skin glow and her eyes glisten. The pants hug her curves in all of the right places and the shoes are top of the line and adored by most women.

Farrah still feels there is something off about the clothes and shoes. She knows that it can't be her because she is aware of her beautiful figure; she looks great in everything. It has to be the clothes. As she is unbuttoning the new blouse to hang it in her closet, a button falls off. That was the confirmation that Farrah needed. Just like she suspected, that look was not her perfect fit. In the eleventh hour, Farrah decides to throw on a dress that had been hanging in her closet and wears a pair of shoes that were stored on her shelf. The next day without good reason, Farrah returns the perfect look.

## Be Better, Not Bitter

**Your unique qualities should never limit your possibilities to be better.**

Farrah is beautiful and she knows it. Men admire Farrah for her looks and her intelligence, which boosts her confidence and her ego. Farrah believes that she is always right; therefore, she is not open to views that oppose any of her own. She nitpicks over inconsequential ideas that her man may have and or the way he cleans, cooks, drives, speak, blinks, or breathes. Most men love a confident woman, but they don't stick around long enough to give her a ring when she is constantly belittling and undermining them. That is what Farrah does and that is why she is still unable to find her Mr. Right.

**When you are determined to display the darkness in others, you will inevitably shed light on the darkness that resides within you.**

No person is the same; therefore, we all have the ability to add something valuable to our relationships. But it is challenging to be valued if what makes you different causes you to think you're too good for your man. Imagine being critiqued by someone you love about your hair, your nails, your clothes, the way you raise your children, and how you cook - how would that make you feel? Do you really believe that you would perform at your best if you were always being judged? Men and women may be different in a lot of areas, but they both have feelings and they both want to be happy.

A man is strong in stature, but he can be just as emotionally fragile as a woman. The worse thing a woman can do to a man is break him down. A woman's strengths are not a man's weaknesses. A woman was made strong in specific areas to be the support that her perfect fit will need.

It's time to shift your focus. You may be great at a lot of things, but you can always be better. Focus your attention on being more of what keeps him in love with you. Additionally, discover your mans strengths and learn to appreciate him for those qualities rather than forcing him to wear shoes that don't fit.

A woman like Farrah is not your typical single woman. This kind of woman is relentless in her pursuit to find her Mr. Right and she refuses to settle with anyone who does not meet her lofty standards. Having high standards is encouraged and it's commendable when you stick to them, but beware of making them unreachable. Is it really important that you find a man who will agree to washing your car two times a week over a man that shows you respect and loves you in spite of your faults? What about finding someone who is God-fearing, kind, giving, respectful, considerate, compassionate, generous, funny, charming, and then some. Your unattainable standards are inevitably going to hinder your chances of a healthy and loving relationship. Allow men to come as they are while they are meeting your list of *sensible* standards.

To add to Farrah's idiosyncrasies, she is afraid to be vulnerable. She is insistent on being perceived as perfect by the men that she dates; however, this need for perfection is prohibiting her from opening up in her relationships. She hides behind a flawless image and projects her unrealistic expectations onto these men. As a result of her behavior, neither person in the relationship is able to get to know each other for who they really are.

If Farrah reminds you of yourself, understand that there are not many men who are willing to stick around to be subjected to your insensitive opinions. In the interest of being in a relationship that allows you to make your Mr. Right happy, you must be willing to accept him for who he is. The only way to fulfill your Mr. Right is to get to know him flaws and all. Furthermore, discover your shortcomings. Attempting to avoid the undesirable sides of yourself or your man, will handicap your connection. Staying true to this perfect persona is stifling; it's hard for you to find a man, it's difficult for you to make decisions, and you constantly search for the wrong in everything. Live the life that you dream of. Laugh when he tells a corny joke instead of picking apart his grammar. Go with your heart and stop relying on the opinions of your friends. Be mindful of not allowing your fear of being vulnerable to ruin your victory in love.

1.  Do you always find yourself looking for something better than what you have?

_____

_____

_____

_____

_____

_____

2. What are some positive character traits that you possess?

_____

_____

_____

_____

_____

_____

_____

_____

3. List some ways these traits have had or can have a negative impact on your relationship.

_____

_____

_____

_____

_____

_____

_____

4. What are some standards you have when in search for
your Mr. Right?

_____

_____

_____

_____

_____

_____

_____

5. Have your standards helped you find your Mr. Right? If not, why do you think that is?

_____

_____

_____

_____

_____

_____

6. Do you think having standards that are too high can result in being single longer than you would like?

_____

_____

_____

_____

_____

_____

Chapter 8

*As* flawed as you may appear to yourself, family and friends, remain faithful - the process will present progress.

# 8

## Style Swap

As we evolve to become better, naturally, we achieve self-awareness. The behaviors we were once accustomed to expressing begin to seem childish and we gravitate toward new approaches on old matters. Think of it this way: Every season there is a new fashion trend. These ever-changing fashion trends inevitably challenge your sense of style. As you become more comfortable with the clothes that complement your style, you learn how to fit the new trends into your wardrobe. Discovering your unique sense of style may not happen quickly, but if you are willing to realize which clothes make you feel the most comfortable, the prettiest, and the sexiest, you will invest the effort.

In chapter four, we provided an exercise to assist you in releasing your baggage. The first step in the process was to acknowledge your baggage and then you needed to identify what provokes the feeling(s) attached. If you have attained success with those two steps, it is time to take out the trash.

## Take Out The Trash

Do you remember as a little girl, sitting with your mom, grandmother, or auntie while they go through all of your clothes from last school year? They were trying to determine what clothes still fit you and what clothes they needed to give away. That is what you need to do: re-evaluate all of the notes that you have taken, the lists you may have created, and the answers to the questions; determine what has gotten in your way of finding your Mr. Right; and throw it all away. What you used in the past during your search for love or even in your relationships, is no longer useful. It is time to go shopping for a new attitude.

## The Solution To Your Evolution

Our goal is to get you to the point where shopping for love is hassle-free. Unlike Tracey who feels pressured to make a decision and impulse shops, you can find the beauty in patience. You will be so different from Erica regarding her misconceptions about the right one. You will develop a strong sense of self and come to understand that it doesn't matter what Mr. Right can or cannot bring to the relationship if you don't know what you bring. You will no longer be anything like Farrah. You will remain confident in your strengths, while maintaining an awareness of your weaknesses. More importantly, you will become open to learning new things about yourself that you never considered. To the man that is fit perfectly for you, you will be his dream come true. This perception of you will be attributed to the beauty that you possess on the inside and out.

Usually the starting point is not a pretty place, but to evolve, you have to start somewhere. Your adverse thinking is common. It is normal for life experiences to taint your perspective on love, and it is not uncommon for women to stop believing in happiness. Despite this reality, it is counterproductive to have a dream, yet settle for dejection.

- Choose to eliminate your negative thinking about love.

- Recognize that you may be picking the wrong guys over and over and over again out of convenience.

- Frivolous shopping is wasteful. Pay close attention to the signs. You will know if you are investing in a quality man or just the "bargain of the day."

- Invest in your happiness and do the work it takes to put you closer to finding your perfect fit.

- Picking the wrong guy can become habitual; take a risk, invest your time elsewhere.

If you have read through this book, you have already taken the first step to finding your Mr. Right. This book was designed to show women how their baggage could be getting in the way of being successful in love and it is a brave act to admit that you may be part of the problem. Congratulations!

Please rely on the tips offered in each chapter when or if you come to a bump in the road (and there will be bumps). Being diligent and dedicated to these tips will push you way past the woman you used to be. As flawed as you may appear to yourself, family and friends, remain faithful - the process will present progress. Your evolution will not come overnight, but know that your actions do not define you and your mistakes are lessons that will make you stronger.

# Special Offers

# Special Offers

To be a successful shopper, you must develop reliable strategies. For instance, shopping experts advise us to wear shoes and clothes that are easy to get on and off, like flats and leggings. The purpose of wearing flats over boots, or leggings over skinny jeans is to make our shopping experience hassle-free. How many of you can relate to being an impatient shopper? The kind that doesn't try on anything; you just buy and go. We used to be that type of shopper. We would see a shirt, like it, take it to the register, and carry it home. Nine times out of ten, that strategy failed us for several reasons. First, the shirt would not be a perfect fit; second, the shirt would be missing a button; third, the shirt would be smeared with deodorant or makeup stains from the previous shopper; fourth, the shirt would be an ashy black instead of a bold black; and then, after discovering all of the reasons why the shirt was not the perfect look, we would realize that it's now too late to return it. We should have tried it on; but since we were too impatient to take out an extra three minutes of our time, we found ourselves stuck with a shirt and out of our money. Thousands of wasted dollars later, we changed our irresponsible ways, acquired patience, and began shopping with a mission. These days, our wardrobe speaks authentically to our own personal sense of style, unlike before when we were just acquiring random pieces to add to our collection of clothes and shoes.

Developing reliable strategies to be successful at shopping for love is equally significant to developing strategies for success when you are shopping for clothes. Good strategies are the essence of healthy dating and subsequently, healthy relationships.

This is the moment that you have been waiting for: the special offers, the bonus buys, or the deals of the week. Well, look no further. We've got you covered right here. Before you start shopping for clothes, shoes, and accessories, you scan the racks for signs that will give you more for less of your money. Well, there is no difference when you are out shopping for love. When you have a friend who has found her knight in shining armor, you want to skip right to the chase and ask her how she found such a great guy. You want to get all of the information that you need to find your Mr. Right in less time and with less annoying heartbreaks. In this bonus section we will share the extras that will boost your confidence while you are out shopping for love.

## Window Shopping

Finding love is not a trend that will ever go out of style, so it's only right and fair that when looking for love, you slow down and take your time. There are a lot of stories that started with love but ended in heartbreak. Sometimes it's because either one or both of the people in the relationship was more interested in gaining a title (girlfriend or wife) than getting to know the person they were courting. It is important that you are certain that you love this man enough to put up with his stashed inventory. Some examples are his religious beliefs, children, children's parents, finances, friends, parents, etc. In your search for love, keep in mind, it is not important to snag the most attractive person or the most financially stable if those qualities are his biggest contribution to the relationship. And equally important, it is not enough to call a person the love of your life if external and materialistic attributes are their best feature.

Know what you want! Yes, this book uses shopping as a metaphor for looking for love, but don't be confused by this theme. Remember that you are shopping for a perfect person, not a perfect pair of pants. This person has feelings, goals, and ambitions, just like you. They are not constructed from a pattern and held together with precise stitching or fancy buttons. You cannot change them by adding sequins. Know that you cannot change them at all! This perfect fit that you hope to find is human and he should be treated as such. Just as unfair as it is to you to rush into a relationship, it is equally unfair to the man as he may not be aware of your motives. In life, some tasks present urgency, but don't rush into finding love. Pace yourself. Make sure you are ready to be vulnerable and devoted to your perfect fit.

Here are some tips to keep in mind when you are window shopping:

- Know your purpose.

- Put yourself in the company of the type of man you wish to attract.

- Stop and carefully observe the man that you think you may be interested in before you fall head over heels with the idea of who he is.

- Keep looking until you are sure you have found a viable option.

# Shannon

## Returns/ Exchanges

I have a friend who relied on her girlfriends' opinions when it came to matters of the heart rather than trusting her own intuition. Of course, all of her friends thought that she finally found herself a keeper. Well, after a few years of dating the guy regarded as her Prince Charming, she started to discover all of the things that she felt were off about him. His aggravations began to surface and her worst nightmare became a harsh reality. At this point in their relationship, she already had her heart invested and hoped that the relationship would change for the better. She feared that she would hurt him, end up alone on Saturday nights, or worse, be unable to ever find a new man.

Think of my friend's situation like this: You just went out and bought a new dress for the party of the year. The dress was a tight fit, but what woman can't stand a tight-fitting dress every now and then? Excited about your purchase, you gushed over this dress to all of your friends. Excited for you, they request pictures of it. You oblige by sending pictures of yourself in the dress through email and text messaging and they all love it.

You thought you finally found the perfect dress for the party of the year. No one has seen you in the dress; all they have are pictures sent through text or email. To everyone else, it is lovely. A few days later you notice the fit is off and what looked like a tight dress just the other day suddenly looked like your little sister's dress. The dress smashes your butt and squeezes your arms so tight that your armpits are pinched. The dress is so uncomfortable that you can hardly breathe. Which of the following would you do:

A. Call your friends for advice

Or

B. Return that uncomfortable, terrible fitting dress and get a new one.

If your answer is B (which it should always be), great job!

What obstructed my friend's ability to follow her instincts was, she chose to listen to other people, rather than listen to her own intuition. When they all thought her man was her Prince Charming, notwithstanding her own feelings, she continued to date him. They all thought that they knew what was best for her. Her friends felt that maybe her impressions were skewed because he was different from all of the other men she's ever dated. Most importantly, they wanted her to be happy and he was the answer. Her friends had good intentions when they were supporting her relationship, but there was no way in the world they really understood what she was feeling.

Your friends can be the best things that have ever happened to you, but all good things must come to an end. Just like children graduate from middle school to high school, there is a time that you will and should graduate from needing to have a consensus among your friends to heeding your own instinct. As we mature in age, we are forced by society to become more independent. Such as, when you're at your job, you're likely to work alone. This forces you to use your better judgment. We are certain that you all work to thrive professionally, so we urge you to use that same drive to thrive personally.

One reason many women do not trust their intuition is because those women have been conditioned to lower their expectations and as a result, they settle for good enough. Another aspect to consider is maybe you have been infected with the disease-to-please. Therefore, no matter what your heart and mind is telling you to do or how to feel, you push past those feelings to avoid hurting people. Whichever condition you think has affected your ability to make a decision without outsourcing an opinion panel, settling for a man is never a good look. Just like in the example where the dress is too tight, you will become very uncomfortable in your relationship. Eventually, you will start to feel suffocated and trapped. That is what being with someone who is just good enough will afford you.

We've observed that some women treat their wardrobes better than they treat themselves. This has got to come to an immediate stop and now! Just as easy as it is to make the decision to take back an ill-fitting dress, it should be even easier to tell the man that you know is obviously wrong for you to hit the road! Just like buying a new item from a store, when you meet a man that you really like, you will be over the moon with excitement; however, later on you may realize that he was not right for you and that's okay. Let the relationship go once you have realized he is not your perfect fit. Be confident in your decision to exchange a bad situation for a new and better one that will complement you in the end.

- Trust your intuition; you will know if a man is the perfect fit for you.

- Break off the relationship before it gets too deep.

- It is okay to discontinue the relationship regardless of the time that you've invested. Don't be entrapped by the idea that you prepared him for someone else because this too has prepared you for someone better.

- Remember that you are looking for Mr. Right, not Mr. Right Now, so let go without any fears or regrets. There is someone better out there.

- Sometimes the one you want to be with is only around to prepare you for the one you're supposed to be with. Be wise enough to know the difference.

**#ALessonLearnedIsABlessingEarned**

## Talk Is Cheap

How many times have you gone into a store and was talked into buying the ugliest pair of shoes or an expensive purse that you knew just wasn't worth it? The salesman told you how the kitten heels made your legs look sexy, or the color of the purse (a hideous green) would complement everything in your wardrobe. At least twelve times, you asked, "Really?!" You knew those shoes looked like they were made by cave people and the purse was a fashion disaster, but because the salesman had the gift of gab, you were easily sold.

The aforementioned is a perfect example of a situation where you must trust your intuition. Sometimes you are afraid to tell people, "no." Either you don't want to let them down or you're not confident in your decisions. However, it is so important to trust yourself. The world is full of people who prey on the meek. They will manipulate you just to get a piece of your pie. They will turn tricks, create clever lines, and spend loads of money; and once they have gotten the good ole pie, they will leave you in pieces like crumbs on a plate. But if you start to trust yourself more, you will be able to discern the real from the fake. You will become a better judge of character and that will supersede the temptation to settle for a man's company because you will know that you are worthy to be your Mr. Right's companion.

- Don't be seduced by what a man tells you; make him show and prove his words through his actions.

- Take action when a man is not living up to what he says he can be or do for you.

- Set realistic standards and never lower them.

*Michael*

## *Solitude Versus Satisfaction*

**Getting to know yourself is key before attempting to get to know anyone else.**

Which of the two is most important? Is it solitude or is it satisfaction? Let me be the first to tell you that both of them are important and neither is greater than the other. The problem arises when we place more significance on one of the two. The two of them go hand in hand - they work together. In order to know what satisfies you, you will have to spend some time in solitude. In order to spend time in solitude, you'll have to sacrifice wanting to be satisfied. As stated in earlier chapters, no one likes to be alone because being alone is associated with being lonely. News flash: it is possible to be in a relationship and still be lonely.

Solitude is oftentimes looked at negatively. Contrary to what most may think, it's actually a positive thing. It is during this time that you discover yourself. You find out what you enjoy the most, what you dislike, what your flaws are, what your strengths are, and more. It is prudent to date yourself and get to know who you are as a single woman. When was the last time you took yourself out to eat or to the movies? If you don't want to date yourself, then why would someone else want to?

We shy away from being by ourselves in fear of what might be revealed. The concept of solitude as punishment has been embedded in us since our childhood years. Whenever we did something bad, whether at home, school or any public arena, the punishment was solitude. The teacher would tell us to go to timeout. Parents would discipline us by sending us to our rooms. Even if we were out in public when we got into trouble, our parents would let us know that when we got home, we wouldn't be watching any TV or playing any video games; man, that brings back memories. Even adults in prison are put in solitary confinement if their behavior is poor.

The goal of teachers, parents, and the department of corrections was not to be unfair or discouraging. Their intent was to give the individual time to reflect on what he or she did wrong. Your parents and teachers hoped that the time spent in timeout, or not watching any TV, would allow you to spend some time with yourself and reflect on some of your negative behaviors. Removing distractions would afford you the opportunity to deal with your issues with hopes that you would make better decisions going forward. You should thank your parents because in the end it helped.

Solitude is misconstrued because people tend to miss the bigger picture. The principle of solitude is to gain or increase inner peace; to acquire clarity on unresolved issues, minus the burden of carrying troubles that you don't have direct control over. We focus on the punishment and not the principle. It's the principle that helps us understand that solitude isn't punishment. The satisfaction that we find will be temporary unless we seek solitude first. Let's assume that a parent never placed their child in timeout. The temporary satisfaction would be a result of whatever behavior their child is exhibiting in the moment. Eventually, their child will get older and begin to realize that immediate gratification has proven to be unrewarding. In the interim, there will be a slew of trial and error. Solitude prevents this cycle from taking place. In their later years, they will notice the repercussions of settling for temporary satisfaction. In most cases, the result of temporary satisfaction is pain.

The same principle applies to dating and being in a relationship. Would you rather have temporary satisfaction to end up with a broken heart as consequence to not spending time alone? Or would you rather have joy in knowing that you'll be ready to embrace your Mr. Right because of the time you have spent in solitude? Solitude will help uncover unresolved issues within. Don't be afraid of what will be uncovered during this time because it will set you up for ultimate success.

## Know Yourself Better Than Before

Supplies: You will need a pretty journal or piece of paper, your favorite pencil or a pen, a positive attitude, a group of honest and loving family members and friends, solitude, and faith.

1.   Write your truest feelings in a journal. Be vulnerable. Be honest. Lying to other people is not smart, but what's worse is lying to yourself.

Discover what you are grateful for, the people who you are grateful for, your biggest fears, etc. Don't be afraid to seek professional counseling if you need help with identifying where your feelings are coming from and how to go about confronting them.

2.   Research. Ask the people who you are the most transparent with to honestly share their opinions of you. (These people will probably not be your coworkers, neighbors, or the cashiers at the grocery store.) Take what they say inoffensively and tweak your personality where it's needed. Some people are going to share great things about you and others will not. Take all feedback and constructive criticism, and make improvements by turning weaknesses into strengths.

3.   Commit to being the best version of yourself.

## Complement Versus Compromise

While conducting research for this book, we met a woman who shared what her ideal husband looks like. She explained that he would be a man in the medical field with a salary of no less than one hundred thousand dollars. Michael and I found it very shocking that a mother of young children was only concerned about the amount of money a man could provide as a husband and a stepfather. Only his lucrative income qualified him - no other questions asked. It was then that we both understood how easy it is for so many women to compromise genuine love to be with someone who only makes us look good, versus someone who can complement who we already are.

### Complement

How many times have we heard the popular idiom, opposites attract? Paula Abdul sung about it, movies were made based on the theme, and books were written about it. But the common phrase was actually a theory conceived from a sociologist by the name of Robert F. Winch. Although this theory is commonly known as "opposites attract," it may also be recognized as *The Theory of Complementary Needs.* The theory was designed as an opposing argument to Isaac Newton's *Law of Attraction.* As we've all probably learned by now, the *Law of Attraction* suggests "like attracts like," but Winch saw things differently. Winch proposed that opposites attract and people are attracted to those whose needs don't match their own.

Both theories are solid. When considering Robert F. Winch's theory of opposites attract, avoid being tricked into believing that because there is an attraction, the relationship should always be embraced. While trying to determine if you have met your match, remember opposites that do attract should be embraced because you are complemented, not compromised.

Isaac Newton's theory is like attracts like; it is popular belief that you should seek out a companion who shares your interests and goals. Although the belief is convenient, remember that humans are meant to evolve which could cause a change in a relationship that was initiated out of convenience. Be flexible in your relationships to remain whole.

Let's paint the picture that you have found your perfect fit. Two individuals drawn together because of their common interest is an example of like attracting like, whereas the opposites attract theory is implemented because the two of you have your own uniqueness prior to entering the relationship. So now we have two different people attempting to come together as one. While together, it becomes the responsibility of both parties to now complement one another, or bring the best out of each other and add to one another. The coexistence of the two of you is improbable if no one is being complemented.

It is imperative that you not just understand, but also apply these principles in your quest for love. Ask yourself:

A.  What am I attracted to?

B.  Why am I attracted to it?

C.  What am I attracting to me?

We can't get into what complements what and who complements who, that solely depends upon the individuals. The point is ladies, what you are looking for should also be looking for you! Because in the end, you will then complement one another. Where some women get it wrong is during their search they are looking for a man to complete them. I'm sure you have either heard this phrase or said it yourself, "Babe, you complete me." Let this be the last time you say it. Please! The statement suggests that in relationships both individuals come to the table with their proverbial cups half full. The truth is, both individuals ought to come to the table with their cups spilling over with personal satisfaction. That does not suggest that either of you are perfect, but you are coming into the relationship being the best version of yourselves.

## #KeepItOneHundred

**When you are searching for someone to complete you, you're hoping to find someone who is secure enough to cover up your insecurities.**

Women will say things like, "My man has to make more money than me," or "He has to have his own place." That is an example of a woman focusing too much on what the man has because she expects him to make up in areas where she falls short. Take a look in your closet. There is not one single item that you can buy to make your wardrobe complete. Whatever you buy will either complement or compromise your style. Women set themselves up because they have a dream man in their minds, but are you the woman that the man you want is dreaming about?

Ladies, sometimes you have to assess what you are bringing to the table. Sometimes there is too much attention focused on the kind of guy you want. Did you know there are implementations needed in order to maintain what you want? What are you doing to be an asset for your Mr. Right when he has entered your life? If you were asked, "What kind of woman do you think your Mr. Right wants", how quickly will you be able to answer? Don't become preoccupied with finding a man that gives you the world over discovering all the many things you can learn in order to keep your Mr. Right happy. Get ready for your Mr. Right because he may not be too far away. Come to the table at one hundred percent and expect no less than one hundred percent of him. Like Ne-Yo sang, "*I'm a movement by myself, but I'm a force when we're together.*" Mr. Right is going to need you to be an impact; but, if you're not complementing him, then the reality is you're compromising the relationship.

1. What are some traits that you are looking for in your Mr. Right?

_____

_____

_____

_____

_____

_____

_____

_____

_____

_____

_____

_____

_____

_____

_____

_____

2. What traits do you possess that will complement him?

_____

_____

_____

_____

_____

_____

_____

_____

_____

_____

_____

_____

_____

_____

_____

_____

_____

3. Do you analyze what you want your man to bring to the table before analyzing what you bring to the table? If so, why?

_____

_____

_____

_____

_____

_____

_____

_____

_____

_____

_____

_____

_____

_____

_____

## *Count The Cost*

In what ways do you determine what an item will cost you? If you see a particular item that's a must have, what is one thing you check before making that purchase? For the average consumer, the answer to this question will be the price tag. You look at the price tag to determine if you can afford to make a purchase; what a disappointment it is to fall in love with an item and then realize it's out of your price range. The interesting aspect of the price tag is that it only shows what the item will cost you today and not what it will cost you tomorrow.

Picture an item that you love. You look at the price tag and the amount shown meets your expectations at the moment. Later that week, you discover that you came up short and you didn't have enough money for lunch, or not enough money for gas, or no money to hang out with friends over the weekend. You'll find yourself saying, "If I hadn't purchased that item, I would have the freedom to enjoy my finances in other areas." This remorseful thinking happens when you don't count the cost.

How do you determine what dating a man will cost you? His price tag is his charming personality or his impeccable smile that lights up a room. His price tag may also be his nice car, his six-figure income, or his beautiful home. His price tag can also be a negative trait. Maybe it's his bad attitude that you're willing to overlook. Every man that you encounter will have a price tag; it's up to you to determine if you can afford it. The cost of an item is not only presented the day you make the purchase, but it will inevitably be shown in the days, weeks, months, or maybe years to come. While you're shopping keep in mind that every expensive price tag isn't an indication of a quality product. Be discerning before solidifying the relationship because the man may not be worth the suggested retail price.

## The Fitting Room

The fitting room is a place set aside for shoppers to try on items before making a final decision. It's safe to assume that every store has one, but some people really hate visiting the fitting room. The process of trying on clothes can be such a drag and very inconvenient when you have to take off almost all of your clothes each time. We all know our sizes; therefore, we feel there is no need to try something on.

Despite the inconvenience, every piece of clothing is made in their unique fashion, which means that all pieces will fit us differently. In the fitting room, you are afforded the opportunity to make sure that the item you are thinking of purchasing is the best fit for you. You will be able to see if it flows, if it hugs all of your curves, and if it complements your style. Some fitting rooms even have three way mirrors that allows you to clearly see how the ensemble looks, which aids your decision-making.

Ask yourself this: Don't you hate when you have to return an item because it wound up not being the right fit for your size? Metaphorically speaking, the fitting room in relationships is just as important as the fitting room in a clothing store. Before you commit or become vulnerable with someone, try him on first. Get to know him in different areas of life. Don't just settle and make the commitment because you think he is the last good option, especially if you clearly see that he may not be the best choice for you. Consider the fitting room as the process you go through to make sure you're making the right decision before finalizing the deal. Do yourself a favor and visit the fitting room. Don't commit to a man without first trying him on.

## Mannequins

Mannequins are designed to grab your attention in efforts to sell you a certain look. Whether it is jewelry, shoes, or clothes, your attention isn't focused on the model, but more on its look. Have you ever tried on an outfit that you've seen on a mannequin and realized it looked better on the dummy than it did on you?

The smart decision would be to hang the ill-fitting outfit back on the rack and resume your search for your perfect look; and we're almost positive that is exactly what you did. What the mannequin presents is the possibility that this perfectly put-together outfit *could* be the perfect look for you. That does not mean that the outfit *will* be perfect for you.

The lesson behind this is simple: In love and relationships, women tend to come in contact with"mannequins." The mannequin represents the man who looks good to you; someone that you decide to give love a shot with, only to find that he isn't the best look for you after all.

Acquire the wisdom to know that just because a man looks good to you, it doesn't mean that he is good for you.

## I'm Doing Me

The perception of modern day single living is defined as *doing me*: living a life that allows you to be free with your choices without fear of judgment.

This ideology has been adopted by the hearts of a culture broken from bad relationship experiences. The decision to do you is typically exhausted when we are in self-preservation mode. Self-preservation kicks in when you have been in a situation that used you and now you must pull out a lifeline to protect yourself from any more disappointment and hurt.

What most people fail to understand is that your single life plays an intricate role in how successful your dating life will be. However, not knowing how to be single can result in self-destruction. The problem is when your mind-set is, *I'm doing me*, the only thing you're really doing is an injustice to yourself, making it more difficult to find your Mr. Right because you're entertaining Mr. Right Now. The time that you waste with Mr. Right Now, can interfere with receiving your Mr. Right.

**Mr. Right Now: The guy who only comes around for fun (sex, partying, drinking, etc). You may like him, but are not really interested in taking the relationship a step further because it is obvious that he does not have anything to offer you long-term.**

It is healthy to date, but not at the expense of hindering the success of reaching your relationship goals. What you don't realize is that all of these different connections are nothing more than a distraction from getting to know yourself. Entertaining all of these different men does not allow time for self-nurturing and personal development. You enter into different relationships and leave them just as empty as you were in the beginning. There has to be some constraints or boundaries while you're single or else you will become self-destructive. You must have limitations to maintain discipline; if not, you will find yourself wasting an abundant amount of time and before you know it, your ability to discern love from lust will suffer.

## *The Switch-Up*

**Friends with Benefits: two friends who engage in activities reserved for an exclusive romantic relationship without the intent to become emotionally involved.**

Have you ever found yourself coming out of a relationship and then you meet someone new who says they're coming out of one as well? Here's what typically happens next: One of you (normally the man) will say, "I'm not really looking for a relationship right now. Me and my ex just broke up, so I'm just looking for a friend." The woman reluctantly agrees and then ultimately find herself in a compromising position. This normally leads to becoming friends with benefits. Becoming friends with benefits is is only perceived as acceptable behavior because you both *appear* to have kindred minds based solely on your current circumstances. Friends with benefits can be a very convenient relationship, but not when you are in search of your perfect fit.

How many times have you been in a friends with benefits situation and fell in love? How many times were you the only one wanting more? As a result of your hurt and disappointment, did you leave the guy alone or did you stay committed to being just a friend?

For the ladies who stayed even though you knew you were playing a fool's game, did your attitude start to change? We call this the switch-up.

During the friends with benefits situation most women go through a metamorphosis. They have accepted the harsh truth which is, you will never be his girl. However, they realize the worse part of it all and that is, they aren't ready to leave him alone. So they perform a switch-up.

You are nothing like the girl he used to know. You see, before he let you down, you were happy. Now that you see his future expectations aren't aligned with yours, you have become bitter. As a woman, you should not allow a guy, or a situation, dictate your happiness. If a serious relationship is what you're looking for, then do not settle for anything less. Benefits denied.

**While you prepare for the permanent, don't toy with the temporary. The longer you entertain a fling, the longer you wait on your ring.**

*#KeepFlingingAndThemWeddingBellsWontBeRinging*

Like we said, having friends with benefits can be very convenient, but to whose benefit does it serve when you are just having sex with him? His. The reason it becomes difficult to break away from that relationship amicably is because the commitment is already there. Ask yourself, what is being committed? Be it time, energy, money, or sex — a piece of you is being committed. You are putting your heart in relationship mode and your security on a roller coaster ride. When it's over, do not blame the guy for the unsuccessful finish; you have to point the finger at yourself. You'll be the only one to blame for your unhappiness and disappointment.

Pay attention to your intentions. Why are you steadily meeting and dating new people when you already have a handful to juggle? You know how it is. There is the guy you call for dinner, then the guy you will call to go to the movies with, and the other guy you call to go out for drinks. Oh, and we mustn't forget the booty call.

**Booty Call: an individual that is used only for sex, typically summoned after dark; someone who is unlikely to become a serious companion.**

## Single Ladies

Living single is the same as over-shopping. Being single doesn't mean you should spend time with every man who makes himself available to you. There should be a level of discipline involved that suggests you will not carry yourself in a manner that's unproductive.

How To Be Single:

- Group outings - hanging out with friends takes your mind off of being in a relationship.

- Develop a hobby - open up to new experiences and possibly learn something amazing about yourself.

- Date yourself - take time to get comfortable with being single: go to the movies, treat yourself to a nice dinner, enjoy walks in the park, etc.

- Refine yourself - improve on skills that you already have or work on skills that you would like to bring into a relationship (e.g. praying, organizing, cooking).

1. What are some things you are willing to do while being single to better yourself as an individual?

_____

_____

_____

_____

_____

_____

_____

2. What are some things you can do while you're single to prepare yourself for a relationship?

_____

_____

_____

_____

_____

3.   When you're single, do you date more than one guy at a time? If so, why?

_____

_____

_____

_____

_____

_____

_____

4.   Are you sexually active with someone you know you are not going to commit to?  If so, why?

_____

_____

_____

_____

_____

_____

_____

## *Maintaining Versus Modifying*

Standards and preferences are two things that we all have when searching for love. Our standards help keep us in line so we're not settling for less than what we deserve, while our preferences aid us in selecting the best option based on who we are and what we like. Standards are highly recommended, but preferences can be the reason some women stay single. Don't be afraid to modify your checklist and step outside the box.

Sometimes we get standards and preferences confused or we think that they are interchangeable. Standards are what you are or are not willing to accept based upon morals and character. Preferences are what a person wants and are oftentimes shaped by what a person likes or dislikes.

Examples:

Standard - You are a God-fearing woman and your potential Mr. Right must be a God-fearing man who dedicates himself to fellowship. With that being said, your standard is that Mr. Right have a relationship with God and attend Sunday morning service.

Preference - You're heavily involved at your church, serve on several different ministries, and attend both Sunday morning services. Your preference is that Mr. Right do the same. Mr. Right however, isn't interested in serving on a ministry. He enjoys going to one service, which is the earlier of the two, and going home afterwards.

If time passes you by and you're still single, it is probably because of your preference and not because of your standard. It's realistic to want to him to be a God-fearing man and attend Sunday morning worship; however, it may be a little more difficult to find the guy that has to meet your list of preferences. The healthy resolution would be to maintain the standard and modify the preference. Still search for the God-fearing man, but don't become discouraged because he isn't packaged the way you think he should be. Don't discredit your potential Mr. Right because of your inability to be open-minded.

## Computer Love

Honestly, the world has gotten pretty crazy and it may be scary dating someone who approaches you on the street or in a lounge. All you have is the "cover of a book." There is no profile attached to his lapel, so you don't know where he lives or works. You don't know if he has children. You have no idea what his interests are. All you have in front of you is a cute face and a smile - and hopefully good conversation.

Fear is not the only impediment when meeting someone. Another factor may be time. People have become more committed to their jobs than their personal lives these days. With prices steadily increasing, there is hardly money or time for a social life. Therefore, plenty of single people have taken to online dating as a resource to assist in finding their perfect fit.

At first, there were a lot of hesitant singles that were not ready to take the bait when online dating was introduced to the world. The concept was so ambiguous and potentially deceptive, but one successful love story after another slowly killed the doubters. Now, there are people that we have encountered that primarily resort to online dating when looking for their perfect fit.

Online dating is just like online shopping. Simply put: you create an account, which includes some personal information and a pic. The personal information that you enter will assist in filtering out the Mr. Right Nows, so that all who is left are your potential Mr. Rights. Therefore, it is imperative that you are honest when answering these personal questions. If you need to take a minute, an hour, or a day to complete the questions then do so. Sometimes we try on various personalities that are really not who we are just because we think it may be a more interesting portrayal of ourselves and that is never a good look. There is a special someone out there waiting for a calm and reserved lady and a special someone out there waiting for a wild and adventurous woman too.

Just like when you are shopping online and you get to see the many options of beautiful emerald green blouses, you are given the same advantage when you are dating online. Online dating sites do not set you up to regret the experience, so you are able to view what the potential Mr. Right looks like. If appearances are important to you and he just ain't your cup of tea, then you can move on without even acknowledging him, unlike meeting Mr. Beast Man in a public place. In a public place (if you are polite) you will feel more obligated to sit and talk with someone whom you know you are definitely not attracted to.

**It's okay if you're attracted to tall, dark, and handsome men, but don't allow a person's outer appearance to totally drive your decision in snagging your Mr. Right. Sometimes judging a book by its cover will have you back at square one.**

Online Dating Advantages:

- Convenience - Online dating is perfect for the busy professional, or the butterfly that isn't so social. Why? Because you are able to shop for your perfect fit at all times of the day, not just happy hour and before the club closes, or when you are shuttling your children around to their many after school activities.

- Affordable - Many of the online dating sites come with a fee to maintain your account, but it is definitely worth the cost if you consider how much money you are saving. Having an online dating account limits the amount of times you have to buy a new dress or pay a cover charge to get inside a lounge to look for your Mr. Right.

- Likeability Factor - Because you create a profile that honestly displays your looks, your interests, and what type of Mr. Right you are looking for, you are more likely to meet someone who has the same interests as you.

- Comparison - Because you are dating online, it isn't that tacky for you to compare your eligible matches. It's not like anyone has to know that you chose one over the other because of looks, interests, or financial status.

Online Dating Disadvantages:

- Deception - This is probably the biggest reason why people shy away from using online dating websites to find their perfect fit. Unlike meeting someone in a public place and seeing him exactly as he is, online dating allows a huge space for deceit. People have photoshopped their pictures, put someone else's picture up, and lied about their entire life in order to attract a companion.

- Too Many Options - This sounds like a good thing and for some people it may be, but sometimes too many options can leave you indecisive. It is important for you to figure out how to narrow your matches down to your perfect fit.

So to all of the risk takers who are eager for something that is new and offers adventure and excitement, give online dating a try! You will never know if traveling down this avenue could work if you don't allow yourself to get lost in love's newest dimension. In the end, it is most important to find what method makes you the most comfortable and confident. What may work exceptionally well for one woman may not work out the same for you. Trust your gut and no matter the conduit of choice, please approach all situations with caution. Have fun and find love!

Think of all the many ways you've compromised your integrity in past and or current relationships. Write a list of standards you want to maintain while you are shopping for love and even after you've found your Mr. Right.

_____

_____

_____

_____

_____

_____

_____

_____

_____

_____

_____

_____

_____

_____

_____

# Standards That All
# Women Should Live By

## *Faith*

This is non-negotiable ladies. And of all the information and tips we shared with you in the previous sections, this tip is the most important. You and your perfect fit should share the same beliefs. Do not cheat yourself spiritually because you met a guy who is attractive, intelligent, and kind. It is unwise to forgo likeness in your faith for a man that only possesses great potential. Later in your relationship, if one of the two of you do not join the other's team, there will be confusion - no doubt. You will be in a disorderly relationship that lacks love for the reason the two of you are always at war. So, wait on your Mr. Right; your patience will reward you the promise of a man with whom you will be equally yoked.

## Friendship

O ftentimes, we think of our partner as a lover rather than a friend. Good sex is paramount in relationships, but you mustn't minimize the significance of being friends with your Mr. Right. A friendless relationship is equivalent to a brewing storm. It has been proven that couples who forgo being each others friend are more likely to experience unfaithfulness (emotionally and physically). Failing to invest the effort into becoming friends with your perfect fit will certainly cause destruction.

Consider the friends that you stopped spending time with due to busy schedules or new romances. The time you didn't sacrifice to spend with your friends caused the gap in your relationships; and when you see them, the verbal exchange is at a minimum. Intimate relationships that lack enjoyment suffer the same. When you either neglect to forge a friendship in the beginning or fail to nourish the friendship you have, the man you once considered your perfect fit will become a perfect stranger. So find a man that you can be friends with; and in your relationship with him continue to be more of his friend than someone that he has to answer to. Take heed to this advice because what you won't do for your man, another woman will.

## Communicate

It is true that if you put to use the tips we have laid out for you, you are bound to find your perfect fit. But don't get it twisted. You are finding the man who is perfect for you, not a perfect man. This means that your Mr. Right will be considerate, accommodating, compassionate, loving, understanding, mild-tempered, fun, charming – not psychic. It is not a known fact to men that they are required to open the car door for their women. It is not understood by all men that they should call their woman every night before she goes to bed. It is not obvious to all men that they should have flowers delivered to their woman's job at least once a year. We could go on and on about the negligence of men, but that is not our objective. Our objective is to tell you that even if your perfect fit is not aware of the demonstrations that you've assumed are a given in relationships, he is not a lost cause.

If your perfect fit embodies most, if not all of the important qualities you hoped for in a man, you are winning. So many women end good relationships over fixable laxities. Communicate your desires. If he really wants the relationship to work, he will conform to almost anything to make sure you remain happy.

## Pursue Your Finish Line

Do you have the idea that you and your husband (or future husband) will be happily married with two kids (a girl and a boy,) and a dog? Or do you see yourself married, no children, and touring the world with your perfect fit? If you already have a finish line in mind, pursue it. Of course, there may be uncontrollable reasons why you will give birth to two boys instead of a boy and a girl. And it may turn out that you have to adopt a cat instead of a dog because your husband is allergic to canines. But aside from the uncontrollable that sometimes enter to remix our happily ever after, it is imperative that you pursue the life that you want.

There have been occasions when man meets woman and the lovebirds hit it off. But later, they realize that they

143

have different dreams. Is it okay to stay? Well, ask yourself that question. Are you willing to be a stay-at-home mom instead of the carefree wife that travels the world with her husband, or is that just too much for you to compromise on? There isn't a right or wrong answer to that question because in every relationship there will be compromise or your relationship will suffer an inevitable demise. Likewise, resentment can bring about suffering in your relationship if you choose to pursue a passion that is not your own. If you are adamant about sticking to what you always imagined for yourself, then wait patiently for the man who shares your vision to come along. And if you are open to making reasonable concessions for the man of your dreams, let that be your choice not an opinionated friend's force.

*Things*
*Remembered*

*I*f you're the woman who has grown tired of the club-hopping knucklehead and have since realized you're more interested in a cultured and professional gentleman, it is unlikely that you will meet him in a dark night club with heavy drinkers and loud music.

*W*hile every woman is entitled to her own ideas of what happiness is, we believe acquiring ultimate happiness in a relationship with your perfect fit is finding that man who complements you.

*S*hopping in stores that sell items that do not complement you is foolish, just like it's foolish to invest in a man who is not worth your time.

*P*romises weren't made to be broken, but when a man toys with a woman's heart, that is exactly what happens.

*T*he decision to limit your demonstration of love for your Mr. Right will be unworkable in that relationship.

*M*isUnderstood is not who you were intended to become; therefore, underneath that pain is a loving spirit lying dormant.

*W*omen oftentimes allow preexisting baggage to block the opportunity for real love to enter.

*To* love yourself simply means to invest in yourself.

*I*t's okay to tell people to mind their business.

*Y*ou must pursue self discovery passionately to have resolve and peace.

*M*isUnderstood is either afraid to deal with her issues or is not aware she is hampered by them.

*Y*ou mustn't be afraid of acknowledging your strengths and your weaknesses - we all have them.

*I*n the world of love to be considered a staple piece, you must be an honest woman.

*L*oving yourself is more than half of the battle.

*W*hen you find your Mr. Right, check your bags at the door.

When you are searching for love and companionship, you should be the only person in control of the outcome.

Don't ask your friend to set you up on a blind date with a guy who's heavily involved in church when all she usually dates are thugs.

Searching for love is not an easy task, but the only way to be successful is to be patient and intuitive.

Lack of patience only produces undesired results, yet so many of us can't fight the need for immediate gratification.

Dating a man that is not your perfect fit is an unpleasant circumstance for any woman.

There is no amount of money, cooking, sex, or lies a woman can tell a man to make him act right.

Whether his heart is in the right place and he wants to seriously get to know you or he is just looking for a booty call, you are the determining factor of where that relationship will go - not him.

*A* woman's strengths are not a man's weaknesses.

*H*aving high standards is encouraged and it's commendable when you stick to them, but beware of making them unreachable.

*I*t is counterproductive to have a dream, yet settle for dejection.

*Y*our actions do not define you and your mistakes are lessons that will make you stronger.

*Th*e connection with a person brings you together; however, the connection to the person is what keeps you together.

*H*onesty is the best return policy.

# Acknowledgements

The word of the Lord says, "*And without faith it is impossible to please Him, for whoever would draw near to God must believe that He exists and that He rewards those who seek Him.*" (Hebrews 11:6)

This process has been a fulfilling experience. We have encountered good, bad, and ugly lessons. But it was God who took us through the bad, carried us through the ugly, and relieved us with the good. It was during the time we spent writing *Mr. Right Meets MisUnderstood*, that we grew in Christ individually, we connected as siblings, and we compromised professionally to win mutually.

In this time we were able to fully understand why it is important to seek Him in all things that we do. And because we've been obedient, He has rewarded us with enlightenment, opportunities, and an outstanding support system.

We pray that our book touches the hearts of women by means that will improve their ways. We pray that our book will assist in bridging the gaps that ruined past relationships. And that our message will restore families to being the hallmark of love, comfort, and stability.

To all of our family, friends, the MRMMU team, and our extended supporters, we send our gratitude for your encouragement and well wishes.

Thank you for reading.

*About The Authors*

## Michael

Michael Banks is one of the most profound and prolific messengers of his generation. As an author, keynote speaker, and spoken word artist, he has been blessed with the ability to challenge the minds of others and inspire them. He will surely leave an impression and have an impact on your life.

"I did some things wrong and I know I can't *right* them all now, so I picked up a pen and decided to *write* them all down."

Michael Banks

# Shannon

Shannon Morgan is best known for being an exceptional creative writer, but on a personal level, she is beyond passionate by showing devotion to her family and friends. With a spirit of humility, she is able to inspire others simply by showing love to all.

"I have learned that living life is appreciating every second, moment, and hour because time is the only entity that is irreplaceable."

Shannon Morgan